MARY, WOMAN OF FAITH

M. Adolorata Watson, OSM

LIGUORI
PUBLICATIONS

One Liguori Drive
Liguori, Missouri 63057
(314) 464-2500

Imprimi Potest:
John F. Dowd, C.SS.R.
Provincial, St. Louis Province
Redemptorist Fathers

Imprimatur:
+ Edward J. O'Donnell
Vicar General, Archdiocese of St. Louis

ISBN 0-89243-260-8

Cover design by Pam Hummelsheim

Table of Contents

1
A Surprise Meeting

A warm relationship between the Christian believer and the Mother of Jesus extends back to the beginning of the Christian era. In our days, this devotedness is being renewed in keeping with the needs of the times. Our dedication to Mary need not diminish, for it is a heritage of strength and beauty that we can hand on to a new generation of Christian people. Devotions change because times change, but our relationship to Mary relies on more than devotional practices. We can know Mary as a woman of faith, a woman of hope, and especially as a woman of love.

Mary, dawn of a new day, is eminently a woman of faith, a model and an example for the Christian of the twenty-first century. These are uncertain times, for we live in the continuing shadow of nuclear threat. At the same time, individually, we live in a kind of security, experiencing change gradually, moving through each day with few surprises, planning our lives and living according to the plans we make. We anticipate what we do not know with certitude. Although security is tenuous, we strive for it. Even though employment at present is particularly unreliable, we become debtors for cars, homes, vacations, and so much more because we rely on the security of present income. We do not look for surprises, do not anticipate them; we accommodate ourselves to the day-to-day living pattern.

Mary probably lived in such a way: a young Jewish woman of her era, going about the business of daily living, drawing water from the well, visiting with friends in the marketplace, meeting the demands of the day as they came.

I picture Mary to myself as a healthy, strong young woman whose home life had given love and endowed her with a sense of responsibility. To the world at large, she was simply another anonymous woman.

In the course of time she became engaged to a man named Joseph, "of the house of David" (Luke 1:27; *see* Matthew 1:16). Engagement for marriage was part of the ordinary course of events. But from that time on

Mary was, to a certain extent, liberated from the ordinary. Hers was to be a life of surprises — some happy, others downright painful.

After the engagement, "but before they lived together, she was found with child through the power of the Holy Spirit" (Matthew 1:18). Matthew's account is more prosaic than Luke's. We enter into the atmosphere of surprise as Luke tells us that "the angel Gabriel was sent from God to a town of Galilee named Nazareth, to a virgin betrothed to a man named Joseph, of the house of David. The virgin's name was Mary" (Luke 1:26-27).

Throughout the Jewish Scriptures, angels are presented as God's visible messengers. We, however, think of angels as pure spirits — if we think of them at all. We cannot imagine seeing an angel any more than we can imagine seeing the workings of our own minds. We are aware of electricity and of our own minds from what they do — the thoughts and shocks that occur to us. We feel that we would be aware of an angel's presence in much the same way. Luke's angel is true to scriptural form and, we are to surmise, looked much like any other man.

I often wonder where Mary was or what she was doing when she was interrupted by this heavenly messenger. Was she beating clothing on a stone to drive out the dirt and restore its original cleanliness? Was she preparing a meal or doing some other kind of housework? Was she pulling weeds or getting ready to plant seeds? Was she resting after a day of exhausting physical work? We can let our imaginations wander as we try to capture the scene that brought Gabriel into her life.

Luke says that it was "in the sixth month" (Luke 1:26), but he does not give us the time of day. Was it at dawn, or in the brightness of noonday? Might it have been at that quiet time of day when twilight was preparing the world for the end of another day? Whatever time or hour it was, truly a new day was about to begin.

No matter what Mary was doing at the time, nor at what time of day the messenger arrived, she was probably not expecting a visit from Gabriel. We can imagine her feelings of surprise and wonder when "the angel said to her: 'Rejoice, O highly favored daughter! The Lord is with you. Blessed are you among women' " (Luke 1:28).

How understandable it is that "she was deeply troubled by his words, and wondered what his greeting meant" (Luke 1:29). This seemingly ordinary Jewish woman was told that she was blessed among women. What did this mean? And what does it mean to us who call her "mother"?

All of us are freely endowed with life by a gracious God, enriched with the gifts he develops in us — formed, called, and groomed to be like him. But of all women, Mary has been treated most graciously by the All-powerful. Only one person is greater: him whom she bore. The angel, alert to Mary's concern and noting that she was troubled by his words, quickly reassured her. "Do not fear, Mary. You have found favor with God. You shall conceive and bear a son and give him the name Jesus" (Luke 1:30-31).

Mary was a virgin; Luke had specifically told us that. Yet the angel told her that she would conceive and bear a son. How, she gently asked, was this possible since she was a virgin? God's messengers were eminently capable of communicating his word to human minds and hearts. "The Holy Spirit will come upon you," replied Gabriel, "and the power of the Most High will overshadow you; hence, the holy offspring to be born will be called Son of God" (Luke 1:35).

Her response was as unassuming as her question had been gentle. No argument, no protestations that such a thing could not happen; it had never been heard of before. Only trust in God could bring forth Mary's response: "I am the servant of the Lord. Let it be done to me as you say" (Luke 1:38).

The words of Genesis 3:15 were now to be fulfilled:

"I will put enmity between you and the woman,
and between your offspring and hers. . . . "

Chosen to be God's instrument in bringing his word to fulfillment, Mary put no obstacle in the way of bringing about the salvation of the world, as she consented to God's will being done in her. She must have been acutely attuned to the voice of God in her life. To hear God speaking in our lives is often difficult, sometimes impossible, so filled with the noise of our times are the days of our lives. From Mary we can learn to listen, to hear what God is saying to us as we journey to our destination.

Interestingly enough, Matthew's account focuses on Joseph's role rather than on Mary's in this unfolding drama of incarnation. One can understand Joseph's concern. Here was this upright young man engaged to a beauty-filled woman. Before they lived together she was pregnant —

but not with his child. Not many Jewish men of that day would have displayed Joseph's gentleness and forebearance. In Jewish society of the first century, man was supreme. An adulterous woman could be stoned to death while a man found guilty of the same sin was left unpunished. Mary's condition understandably raised questions in Joseph's mind. He decided that, rather than expose her to the law, he would divorce her quietly. (*See* Matthew 1:18-19.)

Joseph was to experience his share of the surprise that Mary knew already, "The angel of the Lord appeared in a dream and said to him: 'Joseph, son of David, have no fear about taking Mary as your wife. It is by the Holy Spirit that she has conceived this child. She is to have a son and you are to name him Jesus because he will save his people from their sins' " (Matthew 1:20-21).

We see here something of the role of dreams in biblical accounts. Modern psychology has given renewed importance to these phenomena of our personal unconscious, making it easier to understand an otherwise incomprehensible story. Joseph accepted the dream as God's word to him and "received her into his home as his wife" (Matthew 1:24).

Reflections

1. Life is full of surprises. Unhappy the person who allows life to pass by in the rut of routine, not noticing the unexpected happenings of every day. What are some of the happy surprises you have experienced in living out this day? Other days of your life?

2. We have such limited experience with quiet prayer and reflection that we have difficulty hearing God speak to us. Take time to be quiet, to listen, to hear what God is saying to you. Then jot down what you hear.

2
A Visit of Love

At Mary's Annunciation scene, the angel Gabriel told her that Elizabeth, her cousin, had "conceived a son in her old age . . . for nothing is impossible with God" (Luke 1:36,37). Mary acted immediately on this word and went to be of service to Elizabeth. If any one characteristic of Mary ranks second to loving obedience to God's will, it is compassion for the needs of others. Whether it be a matter of physical need or spiritual support, Mary is ready to be of service.

We can picture Mary, now with child, setting out through the hill country to the town of Judea, to the home of Zechariah and Elizabeth (Luke 1:39-40).

Scripture writers, necessarily terse in their accounts of Jesus, are even more so in what they say of his mother. We are left to fill in the details. Mary, the loving young cousin, *walked* through the hill country. In our days of enthusiasm for jogging or walking, we think of this as good exercise. In that earlier day, it was the mode of travel for the poor. For Mary it was an act of love. How long a journey it was is unimportant. From Luke's account, we know that she went in haste, whatever the evangelist meant by that.

Once again we can let our imaginations ramble as we wonder what time of day Mary arrived at the home of Elizabeth. What might Elizabeth have been doing at the time? Did Mary simply enter the house and call out a greeting? Did Elizabeth, on recognizing the sound of her young cousin's voice, turn in joy and greet her? As Luke tells it: "When Elizabeth heard Mary's greeting, the baby leapt in her womb. Elizabeth was filled with the Holy Spirit and cried out in a loud voice: 'Blest are you among women and blest is the fruit of your womb. But who am I that the mother of my Lord should come to me? The moment your greeting sounded in my ears, the baby leapt in my womb for joy. Blest is she who trusted that the Lord's words to her would be fulfilled' " (Luke 1:41-45).

We do well to make these words our own — to absorb the trust and faith expressed in them. Mary, woman of faith, did not doubt the Lord's words to her. In this sense, surprise gives way to openness to God, to acceptance of his desires. The Lord speaks to each of us daily and in various ways. We want to be attuned to the voice of God in our lives. Perhaps we can find our way to a Nazareth of our own, or to a hill country where we can be free, alert to hear the gentle voice of the Lord in our lives so that we, too, can confidently look forward to the fulfillment of his words to us.

Mary's reply to Elizabeth is the ageless song of joy and trust, of hope for all people of all times. Each one who calls Mary "mother" needs to picture her in the uniquely personal way that makes her easiest to relate to. My image of Mary is that of a vigorously healthy young woman who has completed the trek from Nazareth to the hill country in Judah. Her cheeks glow with color from good exercise. She is alive with the enthusiasm that stems not from a journey ended, but rather from the anticipation of destiny to be fulfilled, of new life begun.

I picture the two women exchanging greetings of affection before Elizabeth could find words to say anything. Perhaps Elizabeth seated herself; but Mary, so filled with the beauty of God's presence in her life, so crammed with joy and gladness, could only pace up and down, crying out:

"My being proclaims the greatness of the Lord,
  my spirit finds joy in God my savior,
For he has looked upon his servant in her lowliness;
  all ages to come shall call me blessed"
(Luke 1:46-48).

My being, she said, the wholeness of who I am as a woman, as a person, cannot be constrained from proclaiming to all the world the greatness of the Lord, my Lord. He has touched my life so deeply that he has found me worthy of his wish for me. His action in my life will cause all ages to come to call me blessed. My spirit is alive with joy in my God.

Did Mary then seat herself across from Elizabeth, look into the eyes of the older woman, and lower her voice to tones of tender love and great wonder? In Luke, we hear her saying:

"God who is mighty has done great things for me,
  holy is his name" (Luke 1:49).

And did Elizabeth take hold of Mary's hand and nod in understanding? Then, after a pause filled with love for so great a God, did Mary rise from where she had been sitting and once again, unable to contain her awareness of the marvels God works in human life, continue her song of praise? To all who would one day share her wonder through the written text of the evangelist, she said:

"His mercy is from age to age
on those who fear him" (Luke 1:50).

We know how true it is that God's mercy tempers the hurts of life for all who love him, revere him, respect him as Creator God. To fear God does not mean to be afraid of our Father. Rather, it means that we reverence him despite the difficulties and sorrows we experience in life, confident that through it all a merciful God will treat us tenderly.

But there was no stopping Mary's song of joy and praise, so completely attuned to the word of God in her life was she.

"He has shown might with his arm;
he has confused the proud in their inmost thoughts.
He has deposed the mighty from their thrones
and raised the lowly to high places.
The hungry he has given every good thing,
while the rich he has sent empty away"
(Luke 1:51-53).

His power in us lifts us to high places of holiness if we allow him space in our lives to work his way, if we are hungry for the food he will give to our spirits, eager to have God in Christ as our daily nourishment, faithful in our search for God in daily living. Unhappily, those who are rich in transitory things will be sent away from the messianic banquet unless they discover a hunger for the Holy One in their lives. The lowly will be raised to undreamed of heights of glory.

Finally, Mary returns to her cousin and, again sitting across from her, in true Jewish understanding of covenant relationship, says:

"He has upheld Israel his servant,
ever mindful of his mercy;
Even as he promised our fathers,
promised Abraham and his descendants forever"
(Luke 1:54-55).

We, too, are descendants of Abraham. We know that God is faithful, that he is mindful of his covenant promises. Mary speaks to us too, through Elizabeth as she ends her song of joyful praise. We are reminded that God is ever conscious of his mercy, and that his promises to us will be fulfilled.

What must have been the further God-talk of these two women as Mary remained with Elizabeth about three months before she returned home (Luke 1:56)? What kind of God-talk might we enjoy were we to speak to Mary about the joys she experienced at the action of God in her life, or about the action of God in our lives? We, too, can discover that we find great joy in God our Savior.

Reflections

1. God enters our lives each day in a variety of ways. He might come to us in the person of a friend or a stranger. He might enter our lives through the circumstances of the day. What are the ways God has entered your life today through persons or through the events of life?

2. Surely Mary and Elizabeth must have enjoyed God-talk. Some of us find it difficult to talk about the action of God in our lives. Others have the desire to talk about God but can't do so because of timidity. Look for ways to enable others to speak to you about the action of God in their lives. Discover how you can communicate to another the work of God in your life.

3

A Son Is Born

Although Mary went to be of service to Elizabeth, Mary's own mission in life went on developing at the same time. The words of the prophet were being fulfilled: "The virgin shall be with child, and bear a son, and shall name him Immanuel" (Isaiah 7:14).

Once again we can try to fill in the details of Mary's life, this time as she returned to Nazareth. Joseph received her into his house. She was protected by him, and she cared for him. Meanwhile, the Word of God was taking shape in her womb — the Word that had been spoken, promised to her when she acquiesced to the will of Yahweh.

Just at this same time, Luke tells us, "Caesar Augustus published a decree ordering a census of the whole world. This first census took place while Quirinius was governor of Syria. Everyone went to register, each to his own town. And so Joseph went from the town of Nazareth in Galilee to Judea, to David's town of Bethlehem — because he was of the house and lineage of David — to register with Mary, his espoused wife, who was with child" (Luke 2:1-5).

How difficult, how different from the journey to the hill country must have been the journey to Bethlehem. Mary was nearing the time for her child to be born. Travel could not have been easy.

Unfortunately, many others also had to go to this city of David. Signs of "No Vacancy" or the like were posted on the doors of lodging places. One wonders what pain Joseph's concern for his young wife caused him. We who have had the experience of sleeping in airports or in bus depots understand the misery of discovering that no place was available in which to spend the night. And she with child!

Whether the place they eventually found was a cave or a stable matters not at all. What is interesting is the bleakness of the account of the birth of Jesus. "While they were there the days of her confinement were completed. She gave birth to her first-born son and wrapped him in swaddling clothes and laid him in a manger" (Luke 2:6-7). She held her child, wrapped him warmly, lovingly, and laid him in the only crib available — a fodder trough for cattle.

Luke portrays the shepherds of the region living in the fields. It was night. Into the darkness the angel of the Lord appeared. We can think of this darkness as the darkness of night and also as the darkness of sin. It was to bring light to the people in darkness that the Word became flesh. The angel said to the shepherds, "You have nothing to fear! I come to proclaim good news to you — tidings of great joy to be shared by the whole people. This day in David's city a savior has been born to you, the Messiah and Lord" (Luke 2:10-11).

We can understand why these poor shepherds were, at first, afraid. They were of no importance to people of power or of distinction. There was no hope for them that they would ever rise to positions of importance in worldly affairs. Yet, they were chosen to experience the glory of the Lord shining around them. They were called to be the first to hear the good news that later would be shared by all the people.

Following the return of the angels to heaven, the shepherds' fear gave rise to wonder, or curiosity. Or could it have been faith? They decided to go to Bethlehem to witness the event they had heard about. (*See* Luke 2:15.) They found just what the angels had told them, the Messiah and Lord, the baby lying where animals fed. They saw Mary and Joseph. And Luke concludes, "They understood what had been told them concerning this child" (Luke 2:17).

Luke gives us no inkling at all as to how they understood what they had been told. We know that, later, Jesus' constant companions did not understand who he was. What really was it that the shepherds understood? They, like us, were ordinary people who found themselves looking at a newborn baby born in exceedingly poor circumstances. Yet we are told that they understood the words of the angel that "a savior has been born to you, the Messiah and Lord" (Luke 2:11).

Perhaps we should dialogue with the shepherds to learn from them.

"Shepherds, what did you see that made you understand the good news brought you by the angel?"

"We saw the child. We saw his mother, Mary, and Joseph standing by her side, and we knew."

"But how did you know, shepherds? He was only a baby, and they his poor parents."

"Do you not understand? Can you not feel divinity reach out from human form and touch your heart?"

"Oh, shepherds, how did the baby touch your hearts? Don't all babies touch hearts that love? How was he special for you?"

And the shepherds answer: "We cannot tell you more than this. What the angel said was true. We saw it for ourselves and we believed. Can you not believe?"

Is truth so hard for us? For some it is; for others it would be difficult not to believe the good news, long promised, now fulfilled. The Lord continues to reach out through human lives and to touch us by his love. Such are the tidings of great joy shared by all of us.

"Mary treasured all these things and reflected on them in her heart" (Luke 2:19). The practice of treasuring the good and beautiful things that happen in life could bring us much joy. So many of us seem to suffer from preoccupation with life's dark moments, quickly forgetting the glow of beauty that breaks over the drabness we often center on.

Reflections

1. The shepherds were surprised by the advent of an angel, then of a chorus of angels, telling them the good news of great joy. Think of some of the good surprises that have come into your life. Treasure them in your heart and see how much more beautiful life becomes for you.

2. Have you been stranded in a strange city because of a tardy bus or a late plane or a slow train? If so, try to put yourself in the place of Joseph or of Mary as they searched in vain for a place of lodging. Feel their sense of need.

4

Joy and Enduring Pain

Sorrow was to be no stranger to Mary.

The task of census registration completed, it seems probable that the parents returned to Nazareth with the newborn child. ''When the day came to purify them according to the law of Moses, the couple brought him up to Jerusalem so that he could be presented to the Lord'' (Luke 2:22).

We might picture a young couple, any young couple, carrying their child as they go to conform to the prescriptions of Mosaic Law. This particular young couple went to present Jesus to the Lord. Joy must have been uppermost as they entered the temple. Joy also was experienced by ''a certain man named Simeon. He was just and pious, and awaited the consolation of Israel, and the Holy Spirit was upon him. It was revealed to him by the Holy Spirit that he would not experience death until he had seen the Anointed of the Lord. He came to the temple now, inspired by the Spirit, and when the parents brought in the child Jesus to perform for him the customary ritual of the law, he took him in his arms and blessed God in these words:

'Now, Master, you can dismiss your servant in peace;
you have fulfilled your word.
For my eyes have witnessed your saving deed
displayed for all the peoples to see:
A revealing light to the Gentiles,
the glory of your people Israel' '' (Luke 2:25-32).

The words of Simeon reveal once again the universal mission of Jesus: ''a revealing light to the Gentiles, the glory of your people Israel.'' He is the fulfillment of the promises made centuries ago in that oblique promise of a Redeemer that we read in Genesis. He is also the glory of Israel, for it is through Israel that the Savior was given to the world, through Israel that the ''new Israel,'' the Church, was born, the revealing light to the Gentiles. With Simeon we bless God for the incomparable and incomprehensible gift of his Word.

Simeon had not completed his prophecy. He turned to Mary and said: "This child is destined to be the downfall and the rise of many in Israel, a sign that will be opposed — and you yourself shall be pierced with a sword — so that the thoughts of many hearts may be laid bare" (Luke 2:34-35).

How startled Mary must have been! What hard, harsh words for a mother to hear. Indeed, not all surprises in her life were joyous. She must have questioned — or at least wondered — why her child was destined to be the downfall and the rise of many in Israel. Mary would have known from the Jewish Scriptures, especially from the prophet Isaiah, that the Messiah would be the suffering servant, would have known that the heart of the mother of such a one would know deep sorrow. Yet, the human heart hopes that the hard things anticipated in life will not materialize, will pass us by.

This first sorrow of Mary would be followed by many others. Young parents today can find strength in the example of Mary when they, too, are faced with sorrow at a child who is born handicapped, or who suffers death in infancy. Each person's sorrow is terribly personal, yet all of us can look to this woman, blest among all others, who teaches us how to absorb the sorrows that enter our lives. Sadness comes, she reminds us, not to destroy us but to turn us to God, to help us become stronger as we face life's hardships, not to be consumed by them.

Others' response to our suffering reveals to most of us, in time, the goodness and compassion that lives in the hearts of those who love us. The outpouring of kindness, of concern, and of consideration truly lays bare the thoughts of those who stand with us in our pain.

The third woman Luke mentions in his account of the infancy of Jesus is the prophetess, Anna. She, too, coming on the scene at this moment of Simeon's prophecy to Mary, thanked God for this gift of love and talked about the child to any who would listen, to all who looked for the deliverance of Jerusalem. (*See* Luke 2:38.)

Jerusalem itself was in sorrow at this time. This "daughter" no longer provided a home for the Israelites but was in the hands of a pagan power. The deliverance Anna spoke about could be read as political liberation, but only if we fail to recognize what kind of woman spoke these words: a woman who "was constantly in the temple, worshiping day and night in fasting and prayer" (Luke 2:37).

This woman of prayer was also familiar with the promises of deliverance from the slavery of sin, the promise of a redeemer, the promise of God's word coming to fulfillment. A people under subjection looked for deliverance, and to them Anna is presented as talking about this child.

Matthew tells us of the astrologers. We are not told how long it was after Jesus' birth in Bethlehem that some astrologers from the East arrived in Jerusalem, looking for him. "Where is the newborn king of the Jews?" they asked. "We observed his star at its rising and have come to pay him homage" (Matthew 2:2). The astrologers received direction and directions from Herod, the ruler of Galilee. The direction was to Bethlehem, but the directions were: "Go and get detailed information about the child. When you have found him, report it to me so that I may go and offer him homage too" (Matthew 2:8).

In this day of detective mysteries, these directions from Herod would have been suspect. His stated wish to offer homage to one who might be his replacement did little to conceal his desire to liquidate his infant opponent.

The astrologers continued to follow the star to the place where the child was. "On entering the house, [they] found the child with Mary his mother. They prostrated themselves and did him homage. Then they opened their coffers and presented him with gifts of gold, frankincense, and myrrh" (Matthew 2:11). These gifts were customary in the Orient as signs of homage.

Again the element of surprise enters Mary's life. What must have been her reaction to this display of respect and reverence for her infant son? We are not told how many astrologers came to see the child, although custom has numbered and named three. But however many there were, would Mary not have wondered at grown men prostrating themselves before her son and paying him homage? They apparently were men of wealth and eminence, with the time and the money and the entourage to make the trip from the East. Also, they were Gentiles.

From his birth, Jesus was welcomed by Jew and Gentile, by rich and poor, indicating that his mission was to all people wherever they were and whenever they lived.

The astrologers, whom we fondly refer to as "the wise men from the East," learned in a dream that they were not to return to Herod. They went back to their own country by another route. (*See* Matthew 2:12.) They responded wisely to the directions given in a dream, but this did not remove the threat that hung over the life of the child. We might do well to ask ourselves who are the Herods in our lives that we should shun by taking another route on our journey, so as to safeguard the Christ in us?

Reflections

1. Parents feel pride and joy when they take their infant child to become a member of the Church through the sacrament of Baptism. Mary and Joseph must have experienced the same type of feelings when they presented Jesus in the temple. Then came the words of Simeon and the incident frequently referred to as the first of Mary's seven sorrows. Enter into her feelings as she heard that her child would not only bring about the rise of many in Israel but the downfall of many as well.

2. Imagine that you are a reporter covering the arrival of the astrologers and that you observe how they act toward the child Jesus. What would you say in your news story?

5

Refugees and a Lost Son

Uncertainty is difficult to live with, and for Mary and Joseph most of their lives were shrouded in it.

After the astrologers left Nazareth, an angel appeared in a dream to Joseph. The substance of the dream was that Joseph was to take the child and Mary and go to Egypt. He was to stay there until the angel advised him differently. The astrologers had spoken of Jesus as ''king'' of the Jews and Herod had no intention of permitting survival to this opponent of his leadership. So Joseph did as he was told and took the child and his mother to Egypt. Not even a hint was given as to the extent of their stay in the alien land. (*See* Matthew 2:13-14.)

We have witnessed enough scenes of refugee pain in our century to understand the trauma, the psychological pain, the emotional turmoil, the spiritual doubts that attack those who are forced to leave their homes, their homeland. The uprooted are forced to live in a state of uncertainty, not knowing whether they will ever reach a safe haven, ever find family and friends again.

For them, Mary, in her second sorrow, set an example. Her trust in following Joseph's directions was not simply trust in her husband; it was also faith in what God was doing in the lives of the three who were his chosen ones.

We can well imagine Joseph waking Mary, telling her that they must leave. Then there were the hasty preparations as they try to think of what they would absolutely need to take with them and what they could reasonably manage without. These decisions made, they wrap the child warmly, leave their house, their land, and go on the road to Egypt.

How many Egypts do we face in our own lives? How many are the evils we must escape in the course of our journey through life? What are the havens we turn to, the friends we count on, the strengths we can call forth from within ourselves? In all our situations of stress we can think of the resoluteness of this family trusting in God.

Egypt was "home" for this family until Herod died. This was to fulfill the word of the Lord as spoken through the prophet, "Out of Egypt I have called my son" (Matthew 2:15; *See* Hosea 11:1).

Of one thing we are certain: God never deserts us. He is constantly calling us home, continuously guiding our ways if we listen to him. We, too, escape the evils that threaten us just as Joseph and Mary and Jesus did.

When Herod was dead, the angel again appeared in a dream to Joseph and advised him that this period of uncertainty was now at an end. He could take the child and Mary and return to the land of Israel because the one who had threatened the life of the child was dead. (*See* Matthew 2:20-21.)

Luke tells us that "the child grew in size and strength, filled with wisdom, and the grace of God was upon him" (Luke 2:40). When Jesus was twelve years old, his parents took him to Jerusalem for the annual celebration of the Passover feast. Whole villages would go together on these pilgrimages.

After the feast, however, the boy remained behind without telling his parents. They started out on their journey, expecting him to turn up among their relatives during the day, but he didn't! (*See* Luke 2:41-44.) Mary's third sorrow engulfed her heart. Her boy was lost!

I think also of the many, many parents whose children are lost in this country alone, children who have run away from home or have been kidnapped.

Imagine the pain that the loss of a child brings to a parent. Only one who has experienced such pain can know the full impact of the uncertainty, the hope and the hopelessness, the expectation of hearing any day that he or she has been found and then the dashing of hopes as the leads lead to nowhere.

Mary knew this kind of sorrow. She can share our pain when and if this should happen to one of us. We need to learn that we can turn to her in our anguish, knowing that she, too, experienced what we now endure.

When they did not find him in their group, they returned to Jerusalem to search for him. On the third day of their search, they found him in the temple sitting in the midst of the teachers.

Into this scene Mary and Joseph walked. They were surprised, to say the least, to see their son in this situation. "His mother said to him: 'Son, why have you done this to us? You see that your father and I have been searching for you in sorrow.' He said to them: 'Why did you search for me? Did you not know I had to be in my Father's house?' But they did not grasp what he said to them" (Luke 2:48-50).

What led them to the temple? Was it that they had such trust in the Lord that they went to pray for guidance in finding their son? How amazed they were to find him there. Jesus must have had a commanding personality, for the teachers listened to him. Did they wonder what kind of boy this was? And were the parents surprised at how exceptional this child of theirs was in his brilliant handling of questions posed to him?

In Luke's account, Mary seems very restrained in her approach to her son. I often wonder what she said to him on the way home. Whatever she said, "he went down with them then, and came to Nazareth, and was obedient to them. His mother meanwhile kept all these things in memory" (Luke 2:51).

This account is the last mention of Joseph in the Gospels. This does not necessarily mean that death came early to him, for there is nothing further about the life of Mary or Jesus either during the time referred to as the hidden years.

Reflections

1. In his fear of rivalry, Herod destroyed the lives of many innocent children. Think of how much senseless killing takes place throughout the world today, how much "wasting" of life goes on in our own country. Then enter into prayer for those who have lost loved ones to acts of violence.

2. Imagine that you can overhear Mary's words to her son on the way home to Nazareth from Jerusalem after the three-day search. What do you think that conversation was like? How does such a consideration help us to see Mary as one of us?

6

Musings and Wanting to Know More

We read nothing further about Mary's relationship with her son until he begins his public life. What was it like, we wonder, for Mary and Joseph to see the child Jesus grow into early boyhood, into adolescence, into young manhood?

He had to be like any other Jewish boy of his day, for he was a fully human person. And Mary, how did she care for him who was at once her God, Word of the Father, and her son, Jesus? Undoubtedly she did what every mother did: taught her son, handed on to him the skills of everyday living, saw to it that he grew in knowledge and love of Yahweh, delighted to watch his changing moods, his eagerness to learn, his joy of life. Days grew into years, and the family knew love and peace.

Jesus progressed steadily, Luke tells us. Progress suggests teachers, primarily his parents. We want to know more, Mary, about your life with your son. You cared for him, your infant son, your boy child, your teenager at work in Joseph's carpenter shop.

You fed Jesus, clothed him, taught him, guided him, told him of your love for him. You told him stories from the history of his people and yours, looked on him with pride as he took his place with the men in the synagogue.

How little we know, Mary, of the days and years between your return to Nazareth with the son who had been lost and those final sad days of his life on earth. How can we learn more about your life during those years? Actually, we can't, but we can at least indulge our imaginations and picture for ourselves how you lived.

We see you making your feelings known to the young Jesus after his Jerusalem escapade. We watch you as you go about the duties of daily life, no different from any other woman at work in her home. We watch the change the passing years bring to you as youthful beauty turns to mature loveliness. We try to imagine what must have been the sound of your voice, the tone of your laughter at the joys of life, the song of praise you sang to Yahweh.

The boy Jesus, grown to adolescence, to manhood, found in you a mother who listened as he voiced his fears or confided his dreams. Obviously you kept in touch with your son after his social activity began and shared the experience of his preaching and teaching, his healing and comforting, his debating with those learned in the Law. We read of at least two of your encounters with him during that period.

Your step, so rapid on the journey to the hill country in your youth, became more steady-paced, perhaps, but always strong and sure. A neighbor in need could count on your ministering help. One who was a victim of sorrow could look forward to your comforting love.

We know that if we allow you to do so, you will teach us something of what it means to live intimately with Jesus, to speak to him of the ordinary daily things of life, to laugh with him, walk and talk with him, to enjoy a meal with him, to love simply being with him.

Reflections

We can allow our musings to take us further and make a journey to Nazareth. Jesus is any age we choose him to be at this time. We walk down the street of Nazareth on a hot summer day. We ask directions, looking for the home of Joseph and Mary, knowing what we know today, but in our dream-like musings being transported back to their time.

On receiving directions, we walk along the street, dust clinging to our clothing, heat taking its toll on our energy. We reach the door, lift a hand, and knock. Mary answers the door, just as we had hoped. We tell her that we are very thirsty, which indeed is true, and ask if we could have a drink of water. She, gracious lady that she is, invites us to come in.

The interior of the house is cool, and we breathe a sigh of relief. It is as we had hoped. She invites us to be seated, then goes to bring refreshment. It is so good to be here, we think, as we find that we are becoming more and more comfortable in this home. Mary returns and offers us a drink of water. We accept it from her whom now in our day we call mother. She sits and visits with us. We discover that it is so easy to talk with Mary. She has a way of drawing us out, so that we tell her about ourselves, confident that she is interested.

As the conversation proceeds, she smiles at one point and asks a question. "Would you like to see my son?" she says. Has your heart ever skipped a beat? It does now as you hear yourself saying, "Would I like to see your son!" Her eyes, rather than her words, seem to say, "I thought so," as she rises and goes to the door of the carpenter shop. She calls, "Jesus! There is someone here who would like to talk with you."

He comes. You see him as you wish, a young boy, a teenager, a man. He advances toward you. Mary introduces him to you, then on the pretext of having to prepare dinner, she excuses herself. She leaves you with Jesus. You have come to him and he has come to you. You experience communion. Mary has brought you together by means of her gentle question, "Would you like to see my son?"

Do you speak first? Or does Jesus start the conversation? Where does he take you on this journey of words? And when you finally leave that home, what thoughts, what feelings, do you take with you? Surely you have discovered how very easy it is to talk with Mary, with Jesus, how simple it is to pray.

7

Prayer and a Strange Incident

We do not meet Mary in person again in the Scriptures until we turn to the Gospel of John. She is at Cana.

Mary was an invited guest at a wedding and Jesus and his disciples were likewise guests at the celebration (John 2:1-12).

In this setting, we discover something of the depth of Mary's compassion and concern. She was an invited guest, but when she noticed that the wine was running out, she went to Jesus and said to him, " 'They have no more wine.' Jesus replied, 'Woman, how does this concern of yours involve me? My hour has not yet come' " (John 2:3-4).

We note with interest that Mary did not pressure Jesus. She spoke to him, listened to his response, then turned to those waiting on table and told them to do whatever he told them to do. We have heard this story so often over the years that we know what happened next. Six stone water jars, each one holding fifteen to twenty-five gallons, stood there. This was prescribed for Jewish ceremonial washings. Jesus told the stewards to fill the jars with water. That done, he then told them to draw some out and take it to the waiter in charge. They did as he had instructed them. (*See* John 2:6-8.)

We can visualize the waiter in charge tasting the water made wine without knowing where it had come from. We can also visualize the expressions of the waiters as they stood there in uncertain expectation. They knew where the water came from; they had drawn it.

"Then the waiter in charge called the groom over and remarked to him: 'People usually serve the choice wine first; then when the guests have been drinking awhile, a lesser vintage. What you have done is keep the choice wine until now.' Jesus performed this first of his signs at Cana in Galilee" (John 2:9-11).

There was no "pomp and circumstance" about this action of Jesus. All was done very quietly, but all was done because his mother had asked him to do so. He answered her prayer.

What confidence Mary had in her son. What an example to us of the power of prayer. "They have no more wine," and "do whatever he says." She is telling us that we need merely tell her son of our need and then do what he tells us. Of course that means we have to listen. Sometimes we are so taken up with our words to him that we have difficulty hearing what he says to us. Mary tells us, "Have confidence in my son."

John tells us that "after this he went down to Capernaum, along with his mother and brothers [and his disciples] but they stayed there only a few days" (John 2:12). So Mary did accompany her son at times during his public life! We tend to think of Mary as staying at home, not being a continuing part of the ministry of Jesus. This passage gives us some insight into what might have occurred as Jesus went about the work he had been given to do. It also raises the possibility of Jesus having spent the night at home with Mary at other times, even though, having left home, he could say that he had no place of his very own.

In a puzzling scene at a later time, Matthew, Mark, and Luke tell us of his mother and relatives coming to where Jesus was. He was speaking to the crowds when this occurred. "Someone said to him, 'Your mother and your brothers are standing out there and they wish to speak to you.' He said to the one who had told him, 'Who is my mother? Who are my brothers?' Then, extending his hand toward his disciples, he said, 'There are my mother and my brothers. Whoever does the will of my heavenly Father is brother and sister and mother to me' " (Matthew 12:47-50; *See also* Mark 3:31-35; Luke 8:19-20.)

When first I meditated on this passage, I thought Jesus exhibited an unfeeling attitude toward his mother. Then I gradually began to understand what he seems to mean — "This woman is mother to me not only biologically, but more precisely because she lives life as I live it — doing the will of my Father. No one has done it more perfectly than she, and those who do as she has done have a close family relationship to me."

Reflections

Imagine that you were one of the guests at the wedding feast at Cana. You saw this little drama being enacted. Later you were telling a friend. Your conversation might have gone something like this:

I have a remarkable story to tell you. I know it's hard to believe, but I was there and I'm giving you firsthand information. I was invited to a wedding at Cana. Mary of Nazareth was there and so was her son with a group of his friends.

I've always felt an attraction to Mary. She is such a charming woman, yet so unobtrusive. I watched her moving among the guests. She was just as I've always known her to be, gracious to everyone, so loving in her way of speaking, beautiful as she smiled at one and spoke to another or listened to someone speaking to her.

You know, I've known this woman for years, knew her as a young girl before she was married.

I was looking at her when the headwaiter offered her a glass of wine. A partly filled glass, I noticed. She said something to him, but I was too far away to hear. They both looked very serious, almost grave. The headwaiter walked away, and I saw Mary look around the room. I could guess she was looking for her son.

When she located him, she moved quickly to where he was. This time I was near enough to hear the conversation, and I heard her tell him that the wedding couple had no more wine. Then he said the strangest thing. He said to his mother, "How does this concern of yours involve me? My hour has not yet come." I wonder what he meant by that?

Anyhow, he wasn't harsh in the way he spoke to her. In fact, there seemed to me to be a trace of a smile on his face as if to say to her, "All these years you have managed to get your way with me. I'm not ready to do some of the things your concern for others urges me on to. Not yet."

But do you know what happened? He did just what she expected him to do. I know you can't believe it, but that man turned water into wine — and it was good wine, too.

Have you ever heard of anything like it? What do you make of it?

Well, reader, what do *you* make of it?

8

Sorrow Great as the Sea

Days move quickly as we make the journey of life. Years become shorter as we go on, or so it seems. Time, inexorable time, carries us along in its wake whether we like it or not. The best we can hope to do is to control our use of it, and in the portion allotted to us, to seek accomplishment of the work that has been given us to do.

Jesus did this. He accomplished what had been given to him to do during his time on earth. He had a baptism with which he was to be baptized, and he moved unerringly toward it. He told his disciples on three different occasions that he would have to suffer and to die. They would not hear of his suffering, much less of his death. His companionship was their delight. But he had to tell them the hard things, too.

Did he also tell his mother? And did they talk together about what must come to him? Did he say to her such words as "Mother, when you agreed to be my mother, did you realize that you also accepted the role of mother of sorrows? You know that I must go up to Jerusalem, be judged guilty of the crime of claiming to be who I am, and then handed over to the Romans to be executed." Did Mary react as Peter had done? Or did she once again say, "Be it done according to his word." We believe the latter.

Jesus, Savior, son of Mary, born to die to give us life, most beautiful son to ever live, Son of God and Son of Man, dearer than life to her who bore him, must now fulfill the destiny that was his from the beginning. The mother who accepted God's will those many years earlier, who gave birth to the Son of God most high, cared for him, and taught him lessons for life, must now allow the salvation of the world to be accomplished, understanding that her heart would indeed be pierced by a sword.

Jesus went up to Jerusalem, he in the lead with his disciples following after. It was almost as if now that the time had come, he was eager for the final work of redemption to be accomplished. All went as he had said.

We can assume that Mary was with the group of women along the way, that she watched Jesus make his painful walk to Calvary. We are present with the women who look on, who see what evil can do to goodness. We look at Mary. Our hearts go out in love to the mother watching her son, now bruised, bleeding, wracked with pain, carrying his cross.

When the top of the hill was reached, the executioners carried out their work. Hands and feet were nailed to the wood, and then the cross was raised. "Near the cross of Jesus there stood his mother" (John 19:25). We, too, stand with Mary. There is nothing this mother can do. She can simply be present to him, show her loyal love as she shares his pain.

For the last three hours of his life on earth, Mary's presence to Jesus was love poured out in sympathy. Yet peace must have shared the room in her heart. She who was so faithful to the will of the Father must have known the peace that can co-exist with pain, for she knew the will of God was done, redemption was accomplished.

Jesus was not unmindful of her presence. "Seeing his mother there with the disciple whom he loved, Jesus said to his mother, 'Woman, there is your son.' In turn he said to the disciple, 'There is your mother.' From that hour onward, the disciple took her into his care" (John 19:26-27).

These words of Jesus speak profoundly of his care and concern for us. He did not leave us orphans in any way. He went to prepare a place for us in the kingdom of the Father, but he also entrusted us to the care of his mother during our earthly pilgrimage by giving her to us and us to her. It is as if he could not be free from the pain of the crucifixion until a last gracious gift was bestowed on all who are his brothers and sisters. He bound us more closely to him, not only by teaching us that God is Father, our father, but that his mother, Mary, is our mother, too.

Quite naturally, we don't content ourselves with merely reading the words of Sacred Scripture. We visualize what took place as well. That is how we find ourselves standing with Mary at the foot of the cross, hearing the words of Jesus to her and to us through the disciple. We witness his death. We stand in sorrow as Joseph of Arimathea and Nicodemus take the body of the dead Christ down from the cross. We see Mary, mother of sorrows, accept the dead body of her Son, unable to perform the task of anointing his body for burial.

Finally, we walk with her to the tomb where he lies. Are not our hearts also pierced with the sword of sorrow as we join those who mourn for this only Son? Do we not enter into her sorrow, feel with her, seek to console her? For now she is our mother, too, and our hearts grieve for the sadness that we cannot take from her. We can only be with her, show our love and loyalty to her. We can only walk beside her, be supportive to her; but we can never penetrate the depth of sorrow that she must bear. Great as the sea is her sorrow, and no one else will ever experience the magnitude of the waves of pain that crest over her and bury her beneath their weight.

Yet it was necessary that Mary plumb the depths of sorrow so as to be our strength in the pain and sadness we must experience during our lives on earth. From her we draw strength and courage, from her we take hope.

The stone was rolled in front of the tomb to block its entrance. It would seem that hope had been buried with Jesus. But what Jesus had foretold came to pass. After three days he rose and his disciples became a resurrection people. Is it possible that Jesus appeared first to his mother after his Resurrection? We have no record of this, but there is so much that is not recorded. It could have happened, couldn't it? Surely he spent time with her before he took his bodily leave of earth. For though our love of Mary is great, it could not compare with the love of the son for his mother.

Reflections

1. Sorrow is a fact of life. No one escapes it completely. As we move through Mary's sorrows in quiet thought, let us reflect on similar sorrows we have experienced or that have come to those we know and love. Our hearts will reach out in loving prayer for all who are in sorrow.

2. We are a resurrection people. We know that sorrow is not the end of life for us. Even during our lifetime, we experience resurrections from pain and suffering. Try to recall deaths that have come to you in your life and the resurrections that followed.

9

A New Day Is Born

One more significant account of Mary is related in Scripture. Luke tells us in the Acts of the Apostles, "Together they devoted themselves to constant prayer. There were some women in their company, and Mary the mother of Jesus, and his brothers" (Acts 1:14).

Certainly those gathered here took time out to eat, to talk about Jesus, to speak of what the future might hold. It seems logical that Mary was the focal person of this talk. How much more she knew of her son than did the others. Who but Mary could tell about the Annunciation, the birth, the boyhood of Jesus? Who but Mary could bring peace to the pain-filled hearts of his friends?

The Church is a people gathered together in praise and worship of God. The Church was being born in that upper room in the days after the Ascension. And on the day of Pentecost, the Spirit of God came upon all who were gathered, filling their hearts and their lives with his presence. The new Body of Christ was born in this room.

Mary, mother of Jesus, was now to be mother of the new Body of Christ, the Church. Surely her spirit was rejoicing in God, her savior. *The Constitution on the Church* says of Mary that she "occupies a place in the Church which is the highest after Christ and yet very close to us" (#54).

In relating to Mary as mother and friend, her life becomes real; our relationship more personal. She is our companion as we move along our journey to destiny. One day she will be present to welcome us to our eternal home, just as she welcomed guests to her home in Nazareth.

Mary, the stranger at your door was welcomed, not turned away. You greeted the wanderer, introduced the visitor to your son, shared food and drink at table with those who came to your home. You teach us to be as we find you: hospitable, compassionate, considerate, sensitive to the needs of others, warm and caring, saving others from embarrassment.

You show us how important servanthood is. You teach us to serve as you served. We see in you a woman who respects herself, recognizes her value as a person, knows that God has done great things for her, and praises him for his goodness to her.

Most of all, you teach us to give birth to Jesus in the dailiness of life, to allow him to live his own timeless life in us and through us. Your acceptance of God's will for you in bringing Jesus into the world changed the face of history. When you said, "Let it be done to me as you say," a new day was born. And for all of this we thank you and we love you.

A Final Reflection

Take any segment of Mary's life, as given in Scripture or as imagined, and expand on it. Write your own "Good News." For example, expand on the story of the birth in the stable or cave. Write about a day in the life of the Holy Family. What part do you see Mary playing in the public life of Jesus? What were some of the stories about Jesus that Mary might have told to the community gathered in the upper room? Or fill in the details of any other aspect of the life of Mary that appeals to you.